SHIFT

Contents

Shift

Butterfly

Shore

SHIFT

Under the Pines

Their fine green packed in to make a dark
and this drew me on
round the lagoon. Paddocks open, swept with sunlight
and the pines
serious as a church.

I still hear their boughs
creaking like steps on stairs in depths of night.
Closer in the needles clarified
and the sound became a mast that might not hold.

To walk off the edge of the green world
and into their dust bowl,
that crypt-like half-shadowed temperature,
and once again
to stand there.

Resin scent rinsed like a sharp shower, tingled long after.
Not moving an inch,
myself to myself become a mystery.

Blood Work

Sheep and cattle arrived by lorry,
the lorries were like yards on wheels.
It was a big deal, my father's work, the smell
was stronger than the brewery.
I took wide paces in my gumboots,
matching his steel-toed stride, I followed him
into the killing room
and spoke my name to the other men.

Nothing stopped, the chain ground on,
sheep hung from hooks, each man with a knife
had his own bit of flesh to deal with.
My lungs ached, my eyes watered
as if there was a fire, the blood everywhere,
red and red over their white cover-alls.

My father handled the aftermath, the sheep
with no head, or feet, or skin, or gut.
Dead cold carcasses coming down a ramp
like fallen angels. He shouldered and stacked.

When the whistle blew
we sat drinking tea from tin mugs.
I was spoken of as his girl,
strong as his strong,
that's when it started
in the blood: *this was his life.*
I felt the join no knife could part
and I couldn't see
how I'd make the journey
going away and away from him.

Distant Fields

ANZAC Parade

Medalled, ribboned chests, an effort
carried through them, the war
still going on inside their heads,
gathered up for roll call.

Where all the flowers had gone
came a quiet of ash,
line after line after line.

As if the grainy footage played above the leafy street
my father lifted me on to his shoulders to see.

My uncles looked to the back of the one in front,
marching to the heart-beat drum.

At end of Mass the bugle rose,
life unto life, a single breath
took flight into the bird-light zone.

The Wash House

The turning on was slower done — the firebox stoked,
the wooden lid the copper had, gilded shine of its deep pan.
And side by side two great stone sinks
for suds and rinse, could hold a muddy child.

The place became a store — chook mash,
pig grits — housed a mat and dust of wares,
played host to mouse. Cat found a hide for bed
and laid her kittens there.

One small window choked with web,
light gave way across the floor; each step
softening to listen hard
though you could never say what for.

Warped tracks of tallboy teased, opened to a world of finds.
A jar of pennies turned to bank. Rust crept
along the blades of knives. And each oilskin coat, from its nail,
stiffened like a corpse impaled. The kittens ended in a sack.

The shedding held small lost endeavour, walls with cracks
poached by the weather, dissolved the meanest acts of time
where garden slept in seed sachets, the mewing
ghosts, the lynching strength of binder twine.

My Sister's Country

Your first cry broke,
barely touching earth
you turned back through the veil
and were gone.

No other girl but you
out before me, almost
weightless, you would not have burdened
an angel's wings.

Sister, what could I be
but an outlaw
against your legacy:
petals unbruised, relentless purity.

You'd scaled to a place
higher than the high country.
I had the crazy dance of a body,
my bones were not ether.

My Sister's Dead Perfection

You were up in the sky,
an absolute star.

You had the ear of God
they said — my God
nothing matched their love
for you dead

nothing on earth
was as pure;
you were the prototype
of girl making good

so I practised reaching
your infinite tall,
jumped from the roof
and the walnut tree

to be perfect too
I thought, I can
be as dead as you.

My Sister Remade

I drew you
back on the blocks of the start,
made you up, filled you out.

In my scheme
you could swear
and say 'no'. I adored you.
My leader

stomping the earth.
You were tough and sweet
and wonderfully mean.

I tugged on your hem
with my questions, I rode
in your slipstream.

Windowpane

The cat rasps her claws on cabbage tree bark,
a note of bird, full chorus done.
Grasses wear a soft embalm. Twilight
could be ripped with engine roar
or the slam of a door, could be
pre-earthquake crackling. At the window
seeing through then seeing *the through*
— waved rippled glass
bubbled, a larger lozenge
you press your eye to:
edges fur, earth and tree,
all the old familiar ground
made queer. You live a moment of between
opened in a distraught glass. The glazier
left a perfect tear.

House

House that went on for miles
to which I return
and the animals return:
dog and lamb, goat and hen.
I touch their coats and feathers,
they feed from my hand.

Floors of linoleum return
my mother buffing in a backward crawl.
And my father returns, stooped
among rows of potatoes,
the ghost of a famine chiding him.

The land of the house has opened
behind the cropped skies of a city
and the sea carried, the sea's echo
along the grey ground of hallway.
The outside filled the inside.

The house went on across miles,
the animals warmed it again,
the dead held it together
ruling in lines of weatherboard
blank to the wind and the beat of the sun.

Saints of the House

They could leave us at any time, being of a substance
thinner than air; they could take us with them,
lifting us out of our sleep, we could be called.

Our good dead shine in heaven. The Devil is a dark horse.
Either way it's not this world. But the Saints are calm,
dreaming the hereafter which is infinite.

I wait for the cracks and breaks beneath my bed.
One life is but a perforation on that long seam,
let not my small soul slip from the covers.

The Walnut Tree

From trunk into the part between
two large limbs, you climbed.
Sometimes wrapped your legs around,
dangled, head mid-air —
turned the world upside down.

Fingered leaves made a screen,
birds housed in the choir stall timber.
Quietly, the walnuts rusted.

And all the method that it took, feeling
bough to bough through your bare foot.
Till far from adult lines of sight,
slowly growing as the limbs of tree,
the start of flight. Elsewhere worked
into view and the living wood held you.

Origin

In the far-away years I dreamt her,
I plied the grasses for a song,
there was no accurate depiction.

Windows of homecoming, plume of a scent
I made it up as I went along,
ignorance bore me over the hills.

I petitioned the wind for a vantage point
as if her eyes would come to me
out of the distance, hazel,
the ones of sun and forest.

Setting Out

Avidly, avidly I went down streets,
I went into bars,
into rooms with strange lighting.

She has been out on her own map
working through junctions,
those enormous roads.

In all the crowded geography
that a landmark hour could come
when we clamour on the door of acquaintance
into each other's arms.

Abroad

I

Your own voice comes back at you
accentuating the rise
as if scaling a staircase of sound,
and everything here goes the other way round.
Everything you say is in question.

II

For the first time in your life
you feel free of your story,
walking street after street
in a city that is layered with history.
You are alone; you are in a zone of millions.
Anonymity shines down on you
from a sky so unclear
after years you will still not know
its true colour.

III

The islands shimmer against damp red brick,
flaunting their best appearances:
wild mountains & rivers & sea.
A tape in your head
plays the earliest memories. *That girl,*
your mother says, *where has she gone?*

The Moss of Bunhill Fields

England, her moisture containments,
quaggy, earth sponge — the old retaining walls
with damp embossed, a towelling green. The moss

anchoring over the burial floor
with a slowness that resembles no movement at all,
the tiny threads squeezing against each other.

Deriders and dissenters, and the plague dead
piled in by the cart-load. The options ended and the futures
— a backdrop grind,
cog-like and electric the square mile soars.

Marooned among the risers, in a hunger for space
pressed on all sides — the stones abide,
pit and crack make for scope as the grey rain falls.

Brings me in to the overlay and underlay,
plane trees and oaks ravishing amid the data lanes and the moss
deep-piled as any clearing-house carpet

— absorbing a restlessness,
between the dead and the living, a quiet matter.

Venice

You knock with your life on the weathered water-doors
believing there's an interior; almond-seller,
glazier, merchants and masons.
The goods you see from the *vaporetti*,
crates of oranges, racks of ice
on which the fish are laid.
And from stern to starboard of a shallow-bottomed craft
stacks of sewing machines, inching under a bridge's arc.

Till somewhere on steps or in an island square
you feel yourself being eluded again
like a hand never made its touch,
or the trance that comes after grief.

Frontier

Walking towards the frontier
Europe rolls out in my mind,
all those shifting lines.
Advance, retreat, troop
and tramp of boots in time.

The line not made by sea:
a country stops, another starts.
Parched palm trees on either side
the tamarisks are just as gold.

As if there were no line
the road sings, it carries
beyond the frontier.

And yet it is a hard line,
intensity between, the soldiers
and the weight, the span.

The checkpoint holds
something in both hands
— release and hope,
the land, the sky and all
the freight of lost belonging.

The Gospel According to Longing

Your skill in complexity, your change of course,
the forest's dark boudoir you navigate,
each new doorway you cross saying, *this time*,
and still I await you; on the balconies
            I take hold of your wrist.

You say you have learnt nothing from life,
that the heart of winter is the same
as the heart of spring. Yet rain falling over the city
is like a hammer, a thousand pianos at the adagio.
My teeth are not smoke,
            I am equal to the wound of any blade.

You tug at the knot. But I have your body.
Here is a breeze from the sea,
      your flesh is my prize.

Angel

St Mary Woolnoth, London

When the sculptor found you
      working this way and that
was it like falling
      back to a time of belief, boyhood,
praying his heart out
as you rose like a guardian from the stone?

Probed by the weather, out-flanked
by fronts of glass and steel,
      it's as if some incredible load
weighed in against your breasts.

Chipped eyes and untapered wing,
      you sleep in the midst
eroding, wondrously unsoured.

Shared Ownership Flat

Housing estate, London N15

I

The young weeping birch sounds mineral,
coursed by the wind, silvering.
It's the closest thing I have to nature —
the upper canopy, a patch of sky
the ever malleable, mobile London cloud
that tells me I am on an island.

What I own here is hard to fathom.
The land is owned by some official body
in the small print; the land itself has vanished
under buildings and car-park.

My neighbours want to go home
to the Caribbean and to Russia.
These are the things we speak about
on the steps outside when something else
has happened — another night, scored
low across the rooftops, one helicopter after another.

II

Summer and the kids are back in the dumpsters
pulling out bits of furniture and busted appliances.
And the young weeping birch, with a whole new
layer of leaf, is giving the wind something to go on.
It's as if the kids were never in the plan,
they haven't a space to exist, except for the car-park,
but they can't resist hunting for it.

III

In the small hours my share shrinks
to a span of car-park lamps,
the birch tree shimmering.
As I try to see what I can count on;
a direction balanced and fed from below,
for the tree it is vital. And being
able to change as the pressure changes
that is the wind's great province,
so fleet, so unattached.

Shift

I

Out of the warmth of Soho
into Oxford Street, among the mannequins
post-midnight, drunk with farewell.

Friends, I miss you all already.
This night brimmed with your hopes,
the South Island couldn't be more far,

as I turn into Marylebone, feeling the hood
of London streets, head in cloud, muffled
each to each, one last hug.

II

Wind and rain, surfing the square,
plane trees, an awning
billows as a sail, umbrellas over the pavement,

whirling round my friend, her raised arm
waving, leaves and rain, tumult
as of a heart, wild beating

then street after street
framed by a cab window, even the most drab
declares itself and I fall

again, the attachment does just sear, London.
Peak to trough of lights like a graph
and from those skyline millions

soft glows to carry
over the Thames. Over the equator.
Too long away to think it does not matter.

Could this become my one *at home*,
among the clouds, the amazing clouds?

BUTTERFLY

Lunch Hour

We spent time in art and poetry
and moved through history and out of fiction
into the street; from the sunlit shelves of Charing Cross
to the hubbub of Leicester Square
I could hear Donne's poem replay in my head:
he has his love and wants the world to go away.

Beside the boles and rummaged leaves
litter bins groaning with summer cans and cellophanes,
there was too much daylight.
The office tugged and tolled
until we stood with a politeness,
phrased from mouth to mouth.

Yet for days I would think of that small aisle
as if an airy room had hovered up above,
I swear her eyes were not looking for an exit.

Butterfly

We entered a year of slow burn
I stole a line from her eyes
She wrote by hand return

The body awoke to the act of yearn
Moisture met the heat of July
We entered a year of slow burn

A door ajar, could yield or close firm
From colleague to intimate ally
She wrote by hand, I wrote in return

Disclosure inched by turn
A long striptease of send and reply
We entered a year of slow burn

Shining and wild were in
Our lines, barely disguised
She wrote by hand in return

All grew from a pact of adjourn
Overwintering, waiting a sign in the sky
Fused on a year of slow burn
Word at the start became touch in return.

First Night

We were high and far away
in a hotel room where
nothing would remember us
or be returned to.

We took each other
quickly — un-tensing
past, present, future
into an ardour of one,

believing our best halves
had been liberated.

Becoming

What was the dream we had on hold
until we held each other, becoming whole? All
that our senses coded
unfolded in our shifts of time and space.

Brooklyn Heights and Lower Battery retraced
as if from outer edges of the city
I could work my way in slowly.
Water gave a quiet that we shared.

The tall doubled on the tongue and trench of waves
till the architecture seemed made of lights alone.
Those nights, New York felt evangelical
turned me around, to walk with you into the thick of it
imagining a re-imagined life; the trudge and tick
and rub, each day coming home to you.

Bologna

What we found there . . .
Osterie and restaurants full
and the rain coming down, I remember,

and the light pressure of her hand
as we ran from the end
of one portico to the shelter of another,
the cobbles streaming.

Nora Reading

She has removed herself as one who reads
removes under a lamp's glow.
Night of her hair, her highlighted cheek
as she leans into the story, her feet drawn up.

Yes, I am watching and listening.
The quiet that is never truly quiet,
close lives and streets,
a helicopter's tracking blades
above, beyond.

The room could be her room
in New York as here in London.
The interior is our discovery
and with discovery comes the desire
to hold it all in place.
This ease of being with her, that is all
and all and all.

Red Hook

Brooklyn, New York

Passing through shadow under the flyover
and from the canal, watching the street part and lift.
The barge, slow as a royal, loaded with scrap.
The jaw in the yard crushing bodies of cars
to cards that were stacked. The neighbourhood
cut adrift; toughing it, shoots sent up through
pavement cracks, tiny green flags in the grit.

Wasn't it ourselves we found there? The old refinery,
loading chute askew, sunk to the riverbed;
big warehouse doors embossed with rusted stars
— the place half ended, half begun.
You said, 'We can see everything from here.'
The harbour plane corrugated with lines
like the streets, written and started again; like our lives,
unravelled and worked, in the red, in the black.

Gaze

Morning carries into the room
sounds of you
wrapped in the shower
as I watch the lines re-ink with light,
mountains so close and vast
as the sea is vast.
Ice a-shine with early sun. The view
. . . something to tell you
as I cross the floor, calling your name.
You're standing, towel at your hair, curtain back,
wet in a gravity of tracks
— shoulder to clavicle;
breasts and belly are a sheen.
I gaze and you
reply to my gaze
as the mountains have never replied
nor the sea.

Umbrella

These are the years when we live on a promise
as migrating birds live
with the knowledge of distant fields.

Even the elephants aim their trunks to the earth
rumbling each other, from herd
to herd. And so you receive

a pulse beamed from a main trunk line,
the satellites switch me through,

riding down floors of the Flat Iron,
background sound: the rotating door
out to the field of Fifth Avenue.

Horns and sirens
and your voice, mouth to ear;
while all around, headlights and tail-lights
track the wet shine.

In a lightweight black coat
and oh, the wrong shoes for rain,
you're fumbling the umbrella's small mechanism

the phone itself is a sort of wonder
as it carries with a rush, the arms opening.

Under Cover

December, Massachusetts

TV on with the sound turned down,
your father under headphones
listening to Schubert or Mahler.
Your mother, two blocks away,
has her own wide screen.
We walk on snow, from one
to the other. Postcard perfect
streets of Marblehead and you
like a messenger, placating,
keeping the peace. 'Home',

Larkin said, 'is so sad',
it ails us as we go.
A window casts red
across a front yard,
an electric solo.
The tallest of trees,
white on green, interlaced.
At ocean's edge, stillness
but for the deep dark
lapping the freeze.

Lapping the freeze . . .
your gentle step
breaks between single beds
and we're almost invisible,
with our hush of unison,
making love like the drowned.

Sunflowers

Van Gogh painted sunflowers for a friend's return
— spilled from a vendor's bucket, the dark-eyed flower
in rapture with the sun. I chaperoned the rough stems
back up the avenue. You were awaited
and the tall flowers had the energy of a torch.

To believe we could have it all — the liberty, your city
while the documents themselves stalled. Attachments
officials specified in great detail; head and shoulder shots:
the resolution, the neutral background.

Yet we were always on our way, always coming back.
Before that future crumpled up as paper in our hands
there was a constancy: gold and all the sisters of gold,
saffron, yellow. The sunflowers lasted on your sill,
                              our heads were turned.

On the Outskirts

Our edge-of-town hotel, pit stop of truckies,
shadowy meetings staged in the car-park.
The foyer had a gloss but in behind
it was so easy to get lost,
the room seemed never where we left it.

The ice machine stood ominous as a lonely suitcase.
Voices stifled. Then bang. A TV suddenly up loud.
Our instincts glued to the adverse and the walls
gave no immunity. The adverse doubled to a gang.

We checked the locks and chain. By midnight
nothing would have budged us through the door
into that bare and winding corridor.

And this a practice run, while our true night
played for time, inked in around us, filling in.
The fear embodied, all our own.
No dawn came to turn that fear benign.

Assignation

The Weather Project, *Olafur Eliasson, Tate Modern*

The helmet of St Paul's ascends in lights,
she walks in through a door of air,
the plane trees are undressing in the rain.

Skeins tack across what's left of dark,
web thickens. Arguing, the body hears
desire through the din, this weather
that's divorced from real life.

We lie upon the floor and wait
for an enacted fog to clear, to see
each other up there on the mirror of a sky.

When I stand the poles of up and down,
right and wrong, are swayed.

A luminosity of grey, she walks
across the concourse, time
become as weightless as a feather

and in the dappling rain she casts a beam
as if there were no other.

The journey-making dream that is the Thames,
the judder and the clang of trains
mounting and dismounting, the bridge between.

Crossroad

I

I can see your face
trying to get through to me
and then it's noon. Feet sliding
on shale of the steep path,
pines tightened against the heat.
Giving up on words is the final failure.

The mountains do not rescue us, or the light
or the tender microclimate of the bay below.
We have it all and are lost.

II

Now it is late, out beside the crossroad
the waiter scoops water along the edge of his broom,
chairs stack up around us.

The last bus has departed, the last meal
has been served; the last time we touched,
when was that?

Silence, as if we'd taken vows.
The tabletop clear, all the way
to where your hands rest.
How long have we been sitting here?

Between

Close in and distant, you had me.
Whichever way you moved
I was swept, arrested.

Between the stay of home
and flight, our poise,
our muddled disarray.

In greys of London light
mid-passage, on our walks
across Brooklyn Bridge

between one country and another
two zones to every hour.
Body into body, that fit,

between the letting go and hold,
your hand all night upon my hip.

You

Who could caress the core,
not founder at its coming,
nightmare with bindings all removed.

Be there for each, be each the other
who made it safe

to speak for the wordless one,
turn innocent ill-gotten shade.

With a touch to wake, a latent bruise,
living ghosts abroad come back.

Sister, friend, lover, much
was misgiven but tenderness
found us also, not always
at a loss; not always unloved, unlovable.

The Dance

The apartment is small, a place of here
and now — two women step into a dance.
There isn't a moon or a star,
no reason at all.

This is our stomp and our whirl
swinging out and back,
this is our twofold orbit,
our rap. We writhe to the drum
and the rip; our moves
as makeshift as ever.

All our said and unsaid
grinds in our tread;
my heart races
like it did at the start.
We dance through the flames
and we dance in the ashes,
we give in this night
with all the sheer chance of our lives.

Prospect Park

Brooklyn, New York

The kids in the park are drawing leaves,
concentrated as they hover over their crayons.
The teacher has somehow calmed her small group
from free time to focus.

Soft plume cloud presses the distance,
grey strains, whittling away
at the taken-for-granted sun. The season bends.
The teacher holds up the hand of a leaf,
edged with sunset, maple.
The kids take it down.

And as if I too could see the day through a leaf,
city not country, the smell of wood smoke
not being prominent in the wide streets
and wide avenues. The park
steps aside from the beat. Gravity having its way
as the wind works the shedding,
all those brilliant colours recalled to earth.

The Big Dark

The town ends and the big dark begins.
Pines and macrocarpas marbled black
in the darkness, some kind of marathon
pull going on in the surf.

The rules are different now; it's not like daylight.
Your feet slide, the shingle grips.
A white wing blurs over lagoon and paddock,
flick of a magician's cloth. Suddenly
you're here without a clue,
bending for air, in a wake of air
trying to breathe

as if combed by the break-line of the sea, as if
the night shore created the acute mind colour
alone, lips pressed to stone,
conjuring: foot, hand, an infinite grind,
a shift from squat to stand.

Lagoon

A navigation has been made,
black swans and spoonbills
come back through all kinds of weather.

Harvest done. Soon they will start again,
rounding the plough, dry summer clods
buried in new dark furrows.

The bristled hills reach for each other
across the gully, creek makes its way there
ends in a pool with this after-sea.

Lagoon is a gathering place, waters
merge; birds find their float
and hutch and settle,

return is an instinct. Things I've known,
hair cut close on a woman's neck, and how they vanish
and how they leave a touch in memory.

Return is an instinct or else it's a wild dream
bending me to this slow water,
scud of foam and kelp,
long flying days unwind

come down. This summer
with its un-companioned course
steers me in.

Hand-drawn Map

Keepsakes

as if something of the past were indestructible,
clearer than a photograph
in scent, in temperature. Our strides

on a brittle carpet seeming to chuckle
across the fall — New England sighed
and another million leaves came drifting down.

Impossible to look back

without looking out from here as I write
in this country that was too far for you,
listening as on a deep blue night

the beach carried its echo up to the cabin.
The setting returns: kauri trees
beloved and rare, the morepork's solo.

The southern hemisphere blew you away
without city, without competing glows
the stars found a stage to dance on.

I recite the heavens alone
where we lay, the earth
under our swimming shoulders.

Small parts of our time together

what the fear has not touched nor the hurt
unravelled, down the avenue of years,
our seasons and the notes left behind

revealing, obscuring — the here-after night sky,
a ground where forgiveness sings?

SHORE

Shore

I

Some days, blind to stone and wing,
more or less moving,
when I am picked up
by the scent again
and am shaken

margin of every elsewhere here.

Back then
I just thought *wind,* I thought
sky — how can I get into it?

I thought nothing would come
if I hung about in these parts for too long

there must be a hinge,
more space than I'd reckoned on

couldn't tell if it was in the horizon
upper sky or under sea

to think of the planet
        enthralled,
I was in its clutches.

ॐ

Spring tides, the reefs
go wild, the surfers
come for the ride —
for what the sea can do
when you stand on it.

Bloom, bloom, the kelp booms.
'Little sea snail
are you fending OK out there
in the brunt of those banners?'

Flower of the ice plant
plumping its cheeks
to the mirror of the sky.
Everywhere — changes;
more touch, more go.

༄

Right mind and how I was never in it,
but not wrong
just some other mind

other, other
sung that verse,
to an anthem, a mantra.

༄

Come home little ones,
        scattered selves,
come home to this nowhere place.
This love.

༄

I tried to show you once
but how could I show you

wings of tomorrow
inside the lupin pod, here

you may shoulder a butterfly
that has come from the inland
to scatter its colour on stone,

touch was a shore
lapping and roaring — a shift in the tide.

A whole landscape made
with the stroke of a hand.

❧

Slim island, slim to itself
and to the world

high-risers in the west
beam their faces at me
— un-resting Alps,

avalanching to the braided rivers.
This is ground of their sending —

the round flat stones of Normanby Beach
lie in their cool grey circumferences

shaped by the journey

is it any wonder?

all wonder it is

arid, ardent, outward seeking
place of first things,

first of each day's light
touches here.

❧

And will the story leave me?
The story will leave you

Is that the going part I will get to?
That's the going, earth says

Even this piece of earth?
Even this
will detach you.

II

Mud all the way, newly ploughed,
my boots in the bog and glug of it.

Headland under a blanket, a grey
brittleness of stalk and stem,
the dunes pulled in on themselves.

When I can't see the distance
I become a listener — surf's reach, the grind
in the undertow — voices, wanting

to get that roundness, to make something out of it.
My friend saying, 'For God's sake
don't go back.' Meaning a regression,

a stop-dead-in-my-tracks
winter — kicking the toe of my boot
against a fence post, to unclog the sole.

❧

Still here
with all
the intangible of a day
              other, other
land borne, air borne, sea turned
— *other,*
come back with my search.
The unfound here, great
gusts of the given.

❧

The southerly boots in, flanked by coal-dark cloud
polar-particled, mean as. Every bit exposed
goes freeze; dragged backward then at the turn
pushed forward. All that stands is on lean
as if on loan, it could blow the hell out of here
as scheme, as plan in my head, blew apart.
Winter's wind-cleaning — marram grass, flax, lupin
— all the living, down to the bone of another fresh start.

ᕯ

Graded to a near plain then steep again
shingle loaded —
we are losing the island by the minute!
Handled and pawed at and abraded
cliff's wet grows wetter, clay
goes sump, goes ooze into fall.

Kelp shovelled in on the swell,
lost footing. Each wave
casting its net and shadow
till the shore feels so fleeting
I hardly know if I'm on board.

ᕯ

Time to move on
those voices say.

The Alps have gone missing.
It's snowing up there.

Solitude wearing thin,
I will become a shade.

❧

What is it that keeps requiting
some untold thing in me?

Shore. Sky. Sea.

Whatever is said
I will not be done with it

— those prints I leave
in the small of the shingle

worked over, the bed
laid open

in which I am taken again.
Belonging was always this,

was always touch,
touch and go.

Fitting

January: the month of doorways and weddings I think
as I lug the monitor up the stairwell, moving in.
The dressmaker down the corridor snowed under with work
and news from England, Stephen to marry Marco.

In a daze of beginning I set the monitor down
and try to fathom why some plugs are working in some sockets
and not in others. I started from here,
this town where column space goes
to Mr Gunther, Mr Smith, Mr Anderson
barking in prose on *bestiality*
... *dirty foul acts* ... *society in the last stages* ....

The building angled where two streets converge
gives the makeshift office a nose, the prow of ship,
scopes a view from the bay to the Alps and back.

With all the space comes scale, somehow I am in it.
The camp table tilts with weight as if the dogmas
come in waves. The current flows and breaks.

Good Day

Timaru

Streetside roses coming out,
each bloom like a beautiful prostitute
tilting her face to the light. All afternoon
we've enlarged our camaraderie,
laughter billowing up from our bellies.

The wide southern sky from Bay Hill
and the Pacific in a clinch
that makes one giant horizon.

We've sat at a table — *the sun fiery,*
the sun broad as a leaf — celebrating
great coincidence under the green warmth.

These two men who love each other, my new friends
who do not shake my hand at departure
but give me a bear-hug. Wonderful!

Portrait in Water

She came home in water,
owned so completely
her smooth easy stroke.

In far seas I thought of her
— the cold Irish sea,
the sun-dazzled Med;
and the lidos of London,
the under-skyscraper lanes
New Yorkers swim in.

All through the rebel years,
each immersion renewed,
though I couldn't swim back to her
yet she was there:
teasing, coaxing and true —

floating me out of my depth
— *it's OK, I've got you.*

The Nor'wester

The Southern Alps are black.
It is February and the rocks are breaking,
paddocks give up their ghosts,
blood slogs in vein. Change
keeps its promise, comes again.

Temperature ascends,
logical arguments of town lawyers
melt into a joke; barometer plunges,
doctors hear strange voices
through their stethoscopes.
The earth feels so upset.

The mountaineers are in trouble,
the windsurfers are in heaven
and our lives are covered
with small dead insect wings
and the ground bones of rabbits and birds.

Paddocks

It's always been a wired country.
Paddocks rebel at their lines,
the wind doesn't stop for a fence.

Swung with erase and revive
I trail the crop's edge, swish
of long grasses that grow there,
feel of the clods break to my tread.

Something has happened to time.
A girl traced the bleached-out blue of the sky,
the sky thickened into a noon.

Paddocks make a bridge
from the near to the far, the sun is on high beam
and I'm looking right into the open.

Wetsuits

One makes five-year plans, the other reads plans
and makes houses. One has the people knack,
as if there were no strangers in the world
but only potential friends. The other
places firm bets; sometimes the horse comes in
and he says it's life when it doesn't.

Two weeks after the funeral,
as if drawing the wagons around
what was left of the family,
their idea of together
was to ride the five-grade rapids
in mourning dark,
bucking a raft down the river.

These are the boys that I grew up with,
men that I love and can never translate.
It's hard for them to talk about things.
They'll never come clean with their tears
but given the chance they'll burn them away
in a snow-fed current and pretending it's play
unload their chests with a scream.

The Powerhouse

Waitaki Dam

The river roared against the cofferdam walls,
the engineers praying
didn't know if the pilings would hold.
The pick and shovel gangs
blacked up with mud
mid-stream in the Great Depression —
barbers and drapers and clerks
stripping it out with the stevedores.

Some years later our father was imported here.
Irish labour, a dynamite man, he broke
and blasted in the last excavations.
An age to every stone; in the ring of pick and chain
did he hear it again — his own father
carting the ballast for Dungloe Pier?

Lonely places ghost the air of the dam,
bald hills and what memory a river has
hauled from its bed — faces
blurred below the water-line, a long time ago.
And that vibration, its eternal hum,
travelling up to the viewing deck
to sound through the railing into my arm.

Morning Fog

Morning an unreadable mask,
slopes the town rested on
stacking uneven roof lines,
every aspect of character
blurred. My father
backed away from yesterday,
memory eddied.
He'd lost the names for things.

Greyness reefs across the inland,
wash of an undercoat off-shore
as if with outlines' decline
it were time for them
to make a last appearance.
There is my mother
in the day-room, feeding him.
She carried one half
of the relation (and what
can we ever carry but that?).

The waves lift and fall,
lift and fall. A child's play
they opened me out from:
hide and seek; the loved one here,
the loved one gone. The town clock
breaks through the muffle.
Birds line up on the pier,
wait for the curtain to lift.

Torch

It barely opens up the dark,
I pilot by its wobbly thread.
The cabin's disappeared, last seen
beyond a distant stand of trees.
I turn back for the way I came
listening to a small owl's cry,
swimming out across the earth,
narrowed to a scope of breath.
Ground cover sounds, leaf and twig
and just the weight of my step
like seeing from some outer space
the 'I' become a tiny speck.

Crossing

The lanes suddenly look deep.
My nephew has a firm grasp,
his little sister loves to leap.

Milk trucks, sheep lorries, endless 4-by-4s.
My eyes, my ears, all muscles wake
as if I could kick the steel that dares.

Left, right (remembered as a rhyme
or prayer) they show me how
to swing my head.

In play, their days are *all that way*,
with disbelief a game goes bust, bump, bang.

And damn it all, they will be met by rough
within life's span and damn it all again:
I have no power to grant a wish
yet wish it still — fend them from spill

to navigate the gaps and make it to the clear.
Lungs fill to invoke useless air!

From one side to the other side,
for all their crossings, may they be steady,
the shores kind.

Swim

I wake up in the morning to push off
from the land. All lovers know
the art of swim, you begin by letting go and being in it.

The wash about my head makes a muddled music
but there's a metronome of breath
and stroke and length.

The possibility of glide, as if I were in practice
for a flight and it's the soul that has me doing laps.

Or else in preparation
for the great reverse — on that long genetic line
that travels through our arms and legs, back to the ape

into the fish — when all the land is gone
we'll be where we started from:
scale, fin, flipper, swim.

At the Station

He drinks from a paper bag, the bottle still in its coat
as he has his own wrapped like a home about him,
sleeping by the old water fountain.
Though nothing runs any more,
not even the trains. Or only the freight trains;
they make the same heavy iron sound.

Maybe he waits for a face to return,
austere as any monk who tries, but cannot shake the spirit.
It's a mean kind of absence, the platform has no give.
Nothing but chance, each day shuffling him into the light.

Process

You tie the sheets together to make one body
you seal the envelope

the leaves brush against each other,
winter comes. You sleep.

In your sleep you gnaw at the envelope
like a lover, pushing your tongue into the folds.

Softly the leaves turn,
night becomes day.

You can no longer see the envelope
only a small pile of sand on the floor of your room.

You reach out your hand in reverence
as if touching the ashes of someone you loved.

Sea Change

Spring and the come-back glow
shifts, blue-green and red-tinged blue,
light hits the undersea bed.
I could lose my footing
on this clay bank, taking my mind
from my step, going over and over
the last time we met. The sun
　　　　roaring in my head.

The High Country

An angel circled above Ben Ohau Range.
Heat radiated from the schist, the air felt migrated.

When it is winter I cannot be here
but it is like winter's echo
immersing in cloudy blue meltwaters,
I shake with clarity and refrigeration.

The wind stirring above the range
and the angel, a parachute with no body.

And when the lonely willow comes to me
I lie under the darkness of it
looking up through a tress of leaves.
I think of my new life that is always arriving

and I think of my dead, who have left the plains
and gone to the place of never-again.

I am forever passing myself like an ancient.
She who is a stranger looks back and asks:
'Are you the one who saw an angel
circling above Ben Ohau Range?'

Thank you to the editors of the following publications in which some of these poems have appeared: *Stand Magazine, Poetry London, Rialto, Ambit, Mslexia, Chroma: A Queer Literary Journal, Magma, Island, Snorkel, Poetrix, Landfall, Takahe, Poetry New Zealand, JAAM, Bravado, Sport, The Courier*, the *Otago Daily Times* and *Before the Sirocco*, the 2008 New Zealand Poetry Society anthology.

I am enormously grateful to the Janet Frame Literary Trust for the Janet Frame Literary Award, which I received in 2008. Thank you to Creative New Zealand for a grant in 2010, which bought time to finish the book. My thanks also to Jane Duran, Alison Rutherford, Bernadette Hall and Gail Trentham for their reading and consideration of the poems at various times.